The New Eighteenth-Century Home

To my parents
M. L.

To Marido, Laurent, and Robin
G. T.

The New Eighteenth-Century Home

Michèle Lalande

Photographs by Gilles Trillard

Abrams
New York

The House that Faces the Mountain

In the 1980s, a young man from Ardèche staked his claim by "going up" to Paris, his head filled with entrepreneurial dreams. Aurélien, who was only sixteen years old, enrolled in a hotel management school, where he developed his social skills and his taste for fine things. But he was drawn to advertising. Out of two hundred candidates, he landed a position as a press agent. He went on to found his own artistic agency, which today includes no fewer than thirty hair stylists and makeup artists. His wife, Pascale, was born in the Pyrenees, between Bigorre and Béarn. It is there that they and their two children put down roots and where they found the home where Aurélien could satisfy his other passion: decor. From an early age, he has loved antiquing. He organizes regular sales, at which the quality of the pieces competes for attention with the sumptuous staging of his finds, all within the construction sites of his decorating practice. This year, he will open his first showroom in Paris.

At the exit to a little village, with the snow-covered summit of Aneto on the horizon, they discovered perfection. Constructed in the seventeenth century for a lay abbot ennobled by Louis XIV and expanded in the eighteenth century by a family of country gentry, this house has passed through time nearly intact.

There, Pascale and Aurélien found enormous rooms, beautiful high ceilings, big windows fashioned out of little square panes, interior shutters with moldings, original floors, an untouched granary, and orangery-like outbuildings that would make pretty residences all by themselves. The restoration was energetically led by village artisans. The walls of the house were entrusted to a wizard of patina: Arnaud Lessaus, who covers the walls in canvas, whitewashes them, then waxes them, thus regaining the shades and textures of old-fashioned rendering. The rest was up to Aurélien: to traipse across the French countryside, and through Sweden as well, to ferret out the chest of drawers, the chandelier, the artifact that would revive each room of the house as if the intervening centuries had simply slipped away. Seasonal rentals and film shoots allow the family to share this exceptional place with others.

On the Napoleon III console table, edged with an eighteenth-century frieze, a painted terra-cotta bust with Italian candlesticks of gilded wood. The engraving illustrates the theme of gourmandise. In a Directoire-period, marquise-shaped faience bowl, a blown-glass cooler holds English silver knives, surrounded by eighteenth-century glass stemware.

In the living room, the original fireplace of Pyrenees marble is set off by a characteristic Provençal mirror from the eighteenth century and adorned with a series of silvered glass candlesticks and a pair of nineteenth-century zinc planters. On the Gustavian secretary, a baluster lamp in Toulouse terra-cotta. The 1940s chandelier has been enhanced with antique drop beads.

On a Swedish secretary with a palm leaf motif, a wooden Italian church vase from the eighteenth century.

In the small salon, an oratory serves as a china cabinet, with a collection of eighteenth- and nineteenth-century faience: Creamware, Pont-aux-Choux, Montereau, Creil, etc.

This fairy-tale bed is embellished with a Polish-style canopy. On the finely embroidered sheets, an antique Provençal boutis quilt in a pale mauve

that harmonizes with the delicate dove gray of Arnaud Lessaus's wall finish.

The china closet was constructed of antique materials, and the wire-grilled doors come from a nearby school. Inside are various pieces of faience, an English teapot, and Parisian porcelain. On the table, an oval faience plate from Montereau

and some marble mortars. The eighteenth-century "ballroom" chandelier has kept its original yellow color; antique drops were added in the nineteenth century. A small birdcage from the early nineteenth century still has its period base.

PREVIOUS SPREAD: *The elegant dining room, its tall original windows framed with interior shutters. On the gray marble mantelpiece, as on the table, Aurélien maintains the off-white palette with antique faïence, both French and English. The spike candlesticks are Directoire era, the fine Italian eighteenth-century chandelier is made of sheet metal, and on the oak console table of the* same period, an upside-down lantern has been wired to support a lamp. The Provençal Louis XV chairs have been left in their raw state.

An Alsatian bench from the early nineteenth century welcomes visitors into the foyer, beneath an eighteenth-century Italian lantern of black-stained and silvered wood.

The music room is papered with old sheet music. On the little rustic table, a chest covered in nineteenth-century wallpaper and a metal violin, a children's toy, with its bow.

In the cupboard, a collection of French and English faience, near a clerical candle-holder in the shape of a heart.

On a workbench-style
side table, two Italian
spike candlesticks.
Nearby is a rare
Provençal chair with
a thatched seat from
between the Louis XV
and XIV periods.

Centered in the
reading room, a
beautiful Gustavian
Swedish pine table
near the Louis XV
daybed. Framing
the mantelpiece, two
generous Louis XVI
bergères reupholstered
in lavender linen.
Under a Regency
mirror, a console table
of the same period.

Before the impressive stone fireplace from the late eighteenth century—which bears the odd device "Neither too near, nor too far"—four planks on a pair of trestles serve as a rustic table, flanked by two farmhouse benches and overseen by a wine-cellar chandelier from the nineteenth century.

Over the cast-iron bathtub, which had been serving as a drinking trough in a nearby field, the alcove is accented by an eighteenth-century sculpted wood pediment retrieved from a bedroom in the house. The pastel is an eighteenth-century portrait of a child. Near the window stands a Napoleon III shaving mirror. The floor tiles are original to the house.

A *Swedish* Manor

Jim and Alexander, both interior designers, live in Stockholm. They also plan extraordinary parties for the royal family, a good part of the Swedish nobility, and the Nobel Prize award ceremonies. One day, they decided to set out in search of an old house from the seventeenth or eighteenth century within sixty-five miles of the capital. It was thus that they discovered this magnificent manor, surrounded by greenery, which met all the criteria they had hoped for: beautiful classic architecture, an imposing roof, low ceilings, and thick walls. They preserved the yellow paint of the exterior walls and the red ocher of the exterior door, a typical Swedish combination. Everything else had to be redone—and so much the better, for interior design is their favorite activity. As a reference to the eighteenth century, they built two little square, zinc-roofed pavilions in two corners of the courtyard to serve as curiosity cabinets. There, objects come and go at the whim of their moods and passions.

At the back of the house, they created a wooden terrace immersed in the natural world. After the first twenty yards, they leave the grass uncut: beyond, it grows in perfect liberty, mingling with the wildflowers, right up to the cluster of trees that surrounds the property. This magical spot is truly the paradise of their imaginings. The interior follows the typically Swedish rules of simplicity and a unified palette: wide plank floors of natural pine, harmonious tones of light gray for the walls, which are sometimes ornamented with hand-painted friezes, ceramic pans from the region, and Louis XVI or Gustavian furniture. Jim and Alexander prefer this inspired period almost to the exclusion of all else. This, too, is the style found in their boutique, Oscar & Clothilde, named after two characters whom they imagine traveling the world and bringing back all sorts of objects, as peculiar as they are inspiring.

The living room
opens onto the terrace,
which was built from
scratch. Nestled under
the trees, it sports
a railing of crossed
wooden beams.

The walls of the
entryway have been
finished with wide
planks painted white
that complement the
choice of black acces-
sories: a polished
Empire banquette, a
pair of sculpted deer's
heads, and a wooden
clock from the region.

The small salon, living room, and dining room form a row on the terrace side. The pair of Louis XVI banquettes is from France. As in the majority of Swedish houses of this era, the floors are of wide pine planks.

In the kitchen, a collection of pewter dishes from the eighteenth century. The metal chandelier, with its garlands of leafy vines, is from the nineteenth century.

FOLLOWING SPREAD: A solemn atmosphere reigns in the dining room. Gustavian chairs finished in black and upholstered in beige Ultrasuede are arranged around a long rectangular drop-leaf table, which is stained black. The parquet floor has been painted to resemble large black-and-white tiles.

In the kitchen, the surface of the table has been stripped and repainted to imitate gray marble. The rustic chairs are from the Gustavian era. In the corner, a pair of storage cabinets in the shape of columns.

In the dining room, a striking buffet and hutch built to resemble a beautiful green-tiled fireplace.

FOLLOWING SPREAD: *In the master bedroom, on a plank-and-sawhorse sideboard, a sculptor's plaster cast of a foot and a reliquary full of hydrangeas. The Gustavian-style frieze was done by hand.*

At the entry to the property, two little pavilions have been added: two follies whose decor changes regularly, in tune with Jim or Alexander's whims and discoveries. Functionless but charming, they are there purely as an exercise in style; one can come here to daydream as evening falls. The pale gray walls are hand-decorated with a light arabesque pattern of foliage. Plaster sculptures, old books, and pastels mingle with mårbackas, pale peach geraniums that are found only in Scandinavia.

A Fair Wind on the

Ile de Ré

Florence is passionate about the realism of her work as a lawyer, but she loves to cultivate her dreams as well. An unrepentant lover of objects and art, she likes to rediscover her pieces by arranging them here and there. Her desire is to understand how a house has lived—to slip into its past and to guide it down new paths.

Seduced by the gentle light of the Ile de Ré, she succumbed to the charm of the simple house. It was already almost fully restored, in a manner that successfully balances the vestiges of the past with the comfort of the contemporary. It has an old eighteenth-century wine cellar, reached through a vaulted door. As soon as you cross the threshold, your gaze sails through the large bay windows to the garden, surrounded by a wall of old stones.

This former working cellar, whose charm has been carefully maintained, forms the living space, including a living room area, with a high ceiling supported by heavy round beams of pine, and a more intimate section, its lower ceiling accented by square beams, for the dining room. Connected to this room, a kitchen has been constructed like a windowed artist's studio looking out on the exterior. A separate building has been added on the perpendicular. On two levels, it shelters huge bedrooms, each one endowed with every possible comfort.

Immediately seduced by the site and proportions of the house, Florence spotted the mark of a great contemporary decorator in the arrangement of space and the choice of fine materials. The work seemed arrested, as if it had suddenly been suspended. She saw immediately how to complete it, how to arrange the furniture, objects, and paintings she had taken from her house in Perche, which she had just sold. She imposed a color palette intended to set off her treasures and to give the house more rhythm, more warmth—a true personality.

With just a few more practical additions, such as an extra shower for those returning from the beach, the house was ready to welcome the family and soon became a vacation home where they visit with great pleasure.

FOLLOWING SPREAD: *On the sofas, two embroidered bedspreads the color of unfinished wood. The low table is a sheet of glass set on four cogwheels. Above the contemporary fireplace, a zinc horse's head that had hung outside a butcher's shop. On each side, two nooks with asymmetrical shelves, where Florence displays the objects she loves: zinc roof finials, dried seaweed, a toile peinte (study for a tapestry), etc. Against the back of the sofa, the side table is a florist's sink, the rooster a weather vane, the floor lamp a prototype spotted at a flea market. Along the low wall under the windows, a figure from a religious procession stands near a doll's chair.*

A wall of windows separates the bathroom from the bedroom, making the whole suite look bigger. The double porcelain sink dates from the 1950s, as does the cast-iron bathtub. On the studio stand, a terra-cotta nude.

In the dining room area, glasses and plates are arranged in a long, simple cupboard, which came from a boarding school. Above it, a carved wooded pediment, an iron windmill, and, in an elegant display box, an unusual collection of leaf insects.

In Florence's bedroom, on a four-level pedestal table made for drying apples, which came from a fruit seller, a collection of nineteenth-century papier-mâché puppets (Sophie Prételat). In front of the window, on the garden table, on each side of the wooden house—probably a replica of a family home made by an artisan woodworker—a pair of lamps made from zinc processional candlesticks.

Under the glass bell, an African woman, sumptuously coiffed, with a three-masted ship of mother-of-pearl, all sculpted out of shells by the set painter Arthur Aballain. On the pedestal table, a Medici vase is filled with seashells. Florence has perched two brightly colored stuffed parakeets there. Below, some zinc weather vanes on the shelf by the fireplace.

Lit by a studio lamp, four naïf-style portraits near a child's penny-farthing bicycle. Near the front door, a wink at nature: silhouettes of pigeons from a carnival game are fixed to the wall.

In this beautiful view toward the guest bedroom, the warm terra-cotta-colored paint on one of the living room walls enlivens the grays and perfectly complements the oak flooring.

Swedish
References

Marlene and Philippe left a beautiful eighteenth-century house that they had superbly restored, hoping after the departure of their children to find a small residence in the city, close to all conveniences. When she visited this house for the first time, Marlene felt a wave of positive emotion sweep over her. With the discerning eyes of an experienced restorer, she saw immediately how to make the most of it. The house dates from the second half of the nineteenth century. It is not very large, but luminous and elegant, with flair, lovely high ceilings, and three French doors opening onto the garden. Its negatives were easy to spot as well: an entry directly from the stairs on the facade, space that was further reduced by Napoleon III arches, and an extremely small kitchen and living space. Since enlarging the habitable space was possible, the solution was obvious. A pavilion, in lieu of a sunroom, was thus placed alongside the house, adding two good-size rooms: a kitchen and a dining room that also open onto the garden through two large French doors, bought through a salvager to maintain the style of the three in situ. Where the old kitchen had been, Marlene created a dressing room; she designed it herself in a circular shape, integrating three old, curved doors behind which she hid the bathroom and changing area. She went in quest of antique wooden paneling for the first floor, imprinting all this space with the eighteenth-century style that she adores above all. And she replaced the archways with wide openings to lend more spaciousness to the procession of rooms. The whitewashed walls add further authenticity to the home.

The four small rooms on the second floor have been reconfigured into a master suite with a softly curved wall complementing that of the stairwell and linking the bedroom to the bathroom. Antique doors found in Normandy, a headboard of salvaged wood, and antique floorboards from an old convent create a Gustavian atmosphere on this floor. It is filled with light thanks to the windows, which have been stripped and left as they are. The bathroom, painted with a lime wash pigmented with iron oxide, displays a restrained elegance complemented with a basin of gray Morocco stone and chandeliers and wall lights were found while bargain-hunting in Saint-Ouen. Marlene and Philippe succeeded in fitting in two bedrooms under the rafters, using antique flooring and doors, two dormer windows bought secondhand, and two bathrooms finished in Morocco stone.

Outside, the surface of the courtyard, which was in a sad state, has been redone in old salvaged flagstones. To give it even more charm, Marlene added a stone fountain and lined the walls with a trellis, which was soon covered with jasmine and climbing roses. In record time, she made this little garden into a cool, secluded haven with an arbor, a wooden shelter, and a shed painted gray to match the house. It is a peaceful little refuge, right in the middle of the city.

The garden is a strong presence in the house, with doors and windows looking onto it from three sides. Each corner is decorated with care: stone fountain, cabinets de verdure, a pedestal table sheltered under an arbor, a painted wooden shed, all conspiring for a sweeter life.

Eighteenth-century pine paneling entirely covers the walls of the living room. The sofa and the medallion portrait are from the Louis XVI era.

FOLLOWING SPREAD: A very soft blue for the taffeta of the living room curtains (Mary Jackson) is picked up in the velvet of the Louis XVI armchairs and the fabric of the sofa. The old fireplace was recentered after the modification of the house plan and set off by a patinated mirror in a brighter blue by Romain Richard, which also furnished some of the woodwork. The corner cabinet, table, and pastel paintings are from the eighteenth century.

The kitchen components, with their brushed oak slats of various widths, blend harmoniously with the house. The three pendant lamps, salvaged from a firehouse, illuminate the garden table, which has had a wooden drawer slid under the tabletop. The hood of the stove is painted a matte black. The look is completed by garden chairs and an Aga cooktop.

FOLLOWING SPREADS: *In the bedroom, the dressing room has been hidden behind four stripped wooden doors. A rounded corridor leads to the bathroom. As throughout the house, a wide-board oak is used as flooring. At the head of the bed, the paneling has been given its finish by Mary Jackson. The two eighteenth-century column-shaped bedside tables, as well as the mirror, come from Annie Kuentzmann.*

A Lesson in *Simplicity*

Every June in Paris, her stall at the Saint-Sulpice fair astonishes visitors with the charm and simplicity of its decor. In the same vein, this eighteenth-century specialist has transformed a fairly ordinary pavilion to the northwest of Paris into a dwelling full of lyricism. Her husband has taken charge of the garden, a peripheral but essential task, for within the middle of the living room one has the impression of being surrounded by the natural world. "I adore the eighteenth century," confides Dominique Pol, "primarily in the form of its popular art. The rustic furniture, with its paint naturally flaked away by the wear of time, tells a story, and fills a house with it. I've antique-hunted with enormous pleasure for many years, but I haven't wanted my house to look too much like my stall. And if the spirit of this great period is indeed present in certain furnishings and details, you will also find some mass-produced pieces."

To permit an equally pleasant life in and out of doors, the facade on the garden side was knocked down and replaced with an enormous window. The same wide-plank oak flooring is utilized throughout the house as needed. With the exception of the kitchen, painted silver gray in order to differentiate it from the rest of the house, all the rooms are white, for they receive light only from one side and must reflect as much as possible. Besides, to create the peaceful milieu that Dominique is so fond of, everything is absolutely white: the sofas, the chaise longue, the light fixtures, all the dishware, every decorative object, vase, candlestick, throw blanket . . . The only color she tolerates is that of the plants and trees that encircle the house like a natural husk.

When they arrived, the garden was just a simple lawn. It has been reworked into different parcels: an arbor, a Japanese garden, a gloriette, a pool with a little wooden bridge. Today, bursting with shrubs, it has all the allure of a tiny, lush jungle, and is far outside the ordinary.

Two steps from Paris, a successful gamble.

Constructed by the master of the house, the pergola with its large wooden logs extends the house into the greenery. White tones create a theme for the furniture, textiles, and objects. Macaroons and imitation cake look mouthwatering despite their subtle hues. . . .

On a chest of drawers
from a dry-goods store,
hatboxes, bobbins of
string, and a dress-
maker's dummy have
all been given a coat
of white acrylic paint.
A set of linen sheets
hides a storage area.

For meals, a table
d'office *with a
terrazzo top, lit by
three operating-table
hanging lamps from
England (X-Ray).
On the easel, a pile
of old books serves as
support for a plaster
artist's model.*

FOLLOWING SPREAD: *Unusually tall windows enliven the wall on the garden side. On oak floor-boards sits an old sofa kept for its comfort, covered with a white sheet and a loosely knit throw (Conran Shop). The low table is made of planks on a metal base. Chairs by Tolix.*

Walda Pairon

The fireplace is a house design. The metal lockers
are factory furniture. Industrial lamp and floor
lamp (Jieldé). Ground lamp (IKEA).

In the armoire, chosen for its very rustic look,
dishes and table linens, all in white.

In front of a photo of Ava Gardner, a console table separates the kitchen from the living area. Made to measure, with its marble tabletop and a metal base, it weighs more than six tons. On top, Dominique sets pharmacy and candy jars, as well as pedestal dishes topped with clear and silver bell covers from restaurants.

A Loft in Kortrijk

"I like to mix things that don't go together . . . ," says it all, or nearly, about Hugues Meurisse. Meurisse, who is from Lille and works in fashion, decided to settle in Kortrijk, Belgium, after falling in love with a warehouse in the middle of town. Kortrijk is a pretty city on the banks of the Leie River. Its Beguine convent, listed as a UNESCO World Heritage Site, is a rarity: forty little white houses with thatched roofs dating from the seventeenth century where a few privileged souls still live today.

With the temperament of a vagabond, Hugues likes to change houses about every ten years and to redecorate every two years. "Guided only by my intuition," he says, "I take no notice of convention, trends, or what people say. I'm crazy about interior design, and I have no preconceived notions at all. The only thing that matters is the feeling I have for the objects." This avowal explains why this loft is like no other.

His goal was to transform this huge building of around 10,800 square feet into an innovative and original house. The architect Stephanie Laporte took up the challenge, attentive to the unusual but precise wishes of her client: to create a universe as crazy as it is sober, a unique frame for a decorating scheme unusual in every way. Three materials and three materials only were employed: concrete, glass, and metal. Simple lines, without a curve, leave top billing to the furniture and art objects of this insatiable collector. Hugues wanted a living room of enormous proportions, open to the sky through a glass roof twenty-six feet up. On either side of this core are two floors and two apartments, one for him and one for his children. Thanks to the generous natural light offered by this glass cathedral, the interior walls of the living room can be black, an ideal backdrop against which to show off old as well as modern paintings, an Italian side table of gilded wood, or a series of colorful busts of Andy Warhol. The result is a true lesson in decoration by an amateur whose favorite hunting ground is the entire world.

PRECEDING PAGE: *In the first section of the living room, eclecticism rules, with a Baroque sofa entirely painted white, both seat and frame, a projector with a Fresnel lens, and, in the glass case, the work of Belgian artist Wouter Bolangier.*

The kitchen can disappear behind pivoting doors. It is discreetly hidden, used only for breakfast. The bathroom is separated from the bedroom by a partition of frosted glass, the sinktop covered in squares of black ceramic tile from Morocco. Opposite, one sees the dining room and the guest bedroom, and glass chandeliers like three clouds floating between earth and sky.

In this spectacular salon, the Gothic oak bookshelves from Alain and Brigitte Garnier set off a collection of bowl- and vase-shaped roof ornaments made of oxidized copper (reproductions of W.R.). The industrial mobile staircase and the coffee table come from Espace Nord-Ouest. Sofas: Conran Shop.

The grand salon, lit by the immense skylight, dominates the other rooms, bedrooms, and dining room. They all receive daylight via transparent glass partitions.

In the dining room, a reworked industrial table. Above the inlaid sideboards, probably Italian communion tables (Arnaud Balusseau, Espace Nord-Ouest), some paintings from last century, from right to left by Tellier, Joubin, and Kvapil.

In the entryway, Hugues has had a Venetian ceiling built in. Along the window, a series of brightly colored busts of the painter Andy Warhol by the German artist Ottmar Hörl contrasts with the golds in the painting and the eighteenth-century Italian side table.

*Framing the entryway, two convivial spaces:
the red salon, to the left, and the parlor, to the
right. In the red salon, the low table is a Portuguese reliquary repainted red, and the Egyptian
"marriage" bergères are gilded in precious gold.
The walls, like the floor, are waxed concrete.*

*The parlor, with bergères and an armchair, opens
onto the exterior through large bay windows.
The painting is a work by German artist
Marie Dassler.*

The Rose-Colored House

A few minutes from Paris one comes to a peaceful village surrounded by fields and, on its outskirts, a house the color of a faded rose. It was once a barn, with a first floor under a granary lit by a few skylights. Its construction date is engraved into the wood of one of the beams: 1687.

In 1950, the barn was converted into a home, and ten years ago, Monique Campuzan moved there with her family. It was an ideal spot for her given that fifteen years ago, she had started her own business with a funny name: Coquecigrues. An amused wink at the eighteenth century, this describes a classical motif found on old toile de Jouy—a sort of flower with the body of an insect.

Since she had always adored antiques and bric-a-brac, Monique decided to reissue the objects she fell in love with: tablecloths, embroidered curtains and lamp shades, mirrors, wall sconces, and any other objects inspired by antique models she finds, often through her friends Colette Jacoillot and Annie Bézard, and which she revisits with a touch of fantasy. Everything is manufactured in India under her personal supervision.

When Monique arrived in her country house, she found a large space of 3,200 square feet, poorly used but with a great deal of character. Thus began a long period of work: with modest funds but ample ideas and perseverance, she was able to reinvent a past that seems perfectly authentic. Salvaging a number of pieces of furniture from her previous house, she gave them renewed youth through stripping and applying new finishes, aided by her friend Annie Kuentzmann.

On the second floor, she laid out her workshop. The monumental framework of the building, with its beams of oak, is spectacular and creates, unto itself, the particularity of the decor. Everything was whitewashed with lime, and all that remained was for Monique to attend to her favorite activity: to make this a place to relax, where one can curl up on a sofa to read or, even more simply, daydream while watching the sky overhead.

FOLLOWING SPREAD: *The main room is divided into three areas, following the rhythm of the beams. In the center, the sofa is covered with a hand-painted linen sheet, bought at an antique shop in Lourmarin. With its back to a screen in the Napoleon II style stands a Tibetan buffet, topped by a painted wooden jewelry box. Nearby, we find an antique mirror and a collection of eighteenth- and nineteenth-century paintings, perched on the beams or hung on the walls or on another screen, unembroidered so as to keep its transparency. Each window is decorated with a fragment of a gilded wooden frame. The armchairs are Regency and Louis XVI.*

A first glance from the threshold of the house reveals a unity of color and spirit in the choice of furniture and the charm of the elegantly curved staircase. Opposite, the small salon: the eighteenth-century table is ornamented with a girandole (Coquecigrues); a railing from an old theater is placed in front of the window. The bookshelf is built of old components. Two Medici vases on a pair of columns guide visitors' steps toward the dining room; the bench is from Provence. The rococo sideboard is from the eighteenth century. On the wall, on top of an old beam, sits a stone garden ornament.

With the chimney and beams as a frame, Monique has used an antique window and glass door to close off the back of the granary. On a Directoire-era desk, a terra-cotta bust of the countess du Barry, under two pastel paintings from the eighteenth and nineteenth centuries.

Above an old table from a cloth merchant's, the lyre and antique candlesticks have served as models for lamps created by Coquecigrues. The painted wooden panel, depicting the dress of a vignotier from the nineteenth century, the pair of wooden wall sconces, and the Louis XVI mirror have all been reissued by Coquecigrues.

On the Regency dresser, in front of a trumeau mirror, a very rare kind of glass candleholder. On the floor, a fragment of a carved and gilded wooden cornice from the nineteenth century, and, on the wall, a sconce incorporating a wooden panel.

On the eighteenth-century Provençal console table, which is partly restored, Medici vases (Coqueci-grues). A canvas painted in the style of a tapestry depicts a romantic park scene.

The same spirit reigns
in the three bedrooms,
with embroidered
sheets, a summer
bedspread, and Cluny
lace for the pillow-
cases and curtains.
All these models are
part of the Coqueci-
grues collection,
including the lamps
and wall sconces.
The oak shelves were
already in the house
and now they are
stripped. Above the
nineteenth-century
bed, a fresco repro-
duced on canvas.

The kitchen maintains a country feel with its Lacanche cooktop. The cabinets are topped with a thick wooden butcher's block. On the wall, shelves, an oxeye window, a zinc frieze taken from a roof, and a coach lamp.

Existing flues were used to incorporate an old Godin woodstove. It is framed by eighteenth-century engravings representing the different traditional costumes of cities in Normandy.

A Dialogue with White

In an apartment built in the Haussmann era, right in the center of Paris, beautiful large rooms are linked by tall double doors left wide open so that nothing arrests the eye. To further accentuate this sense of spaciousness, the walls and ceilings are all white.

On the first floor are the reception rooms, two living rooms and the dining room, the master bedroom, and two additional bedrooms for Maxime and Quentin. Alice and Ines have their own quarters on the second floor. Benedicte took charge of the interior design herself, under the attentive eye of Arnaud. She prefers painted wooden furniture above all, with a particular predilection for Swedish designs. She regularly visits certain Parisian boutiques that she has painstakingly selected; she knows in advance that they will have ferreted out over the course of months everything she needs to add charm to her apartment. For the curtains and the sofa slipcovers, she limits herself to linen, sheer or opaque, because she loves its texture and delicate color.

In this intentionally colorless universe, each piece of furniture, each painting takes on a new dimension.

PREVIOUS PAGE: *This stripped eighteenth-century column has been mounted as a floor lamp (Stéphane Olivier). A painted chest of drawers (Vert de Gris).*

Two sofas with pristine lines for the living room (Julie Prisca). In the bedroom, a small painted wooden bureau and an engraving (Vert de Gris).

On the stone and tile fireplace, a pair of column lamps and an attractive plaster model of two crossed hands under a casting of fruits. On the floor, a horse (Vert de Gris) and candle stand (L'Autre Maison) carved out of wood.

Under a chandelier
purchased on the
island of Murano,
place settings on
a table dressed in
a long white sheet
and a linen table-
cloth. Replicas of a
Gustavian model,
eight chairs (Martine
Colliander for L'Autre
Maison) surround
the table.

In the library, the
Louis XV sofa is
upholstered in taupe
linen (Mary Haour).
The curtains are
made out of bone-
colored sheer linen.
Behind the stepladder,
a plaster cast (L'Autre
Maison).

From the dining room, the gaze is attracted by a luxuriant balcony: bamboo in pots, baskets of fresh flowers, a birdcage. The atmosphere is carried into the room by the pots of ivy and hydrangea.

In the Land of the Midnight Sun

This pretty Swedish wooden house looks like the ones you see on postcards, painted the same distinctive red ocher color, tinted with copper, that creates the charm and unity of this northern countryside. The symbol of this province in the center of Sweden is a small wooden horse in a slightly naif style, painted in bright colors, which is sold in artisans' shops. The original, which is the size of a mammoth, is planted at the gates of the city, on the Leksand highway. Anneli was working in Stockholm, 185 miles from Leksand, but five years ago she opened an interior design boutique with her childhood friend Barbrö and created a line of furniture inspired by the Gustavian style, crafted by artisans using traditional methods. The business grew so much that, rather than expanding, the two friends decided to close their showroom and sell only through the Internet and catalogs, which has in no way impeded the connections they had developed with suppliers.

Fleeing the bustle of the city, Anneli chose to move into her house in Leksand, attracted by the beauty of this spot on the edge of a lake. The decor is based on her creations, mixed with other antique furniture, but always from the Gustavian era. Light streams in all day through long banks of windows along the perimeter. On the ground floor, the main room is devoted to the kitchen and dining room area, which features a big pine farmhouse table from the eighteenth century. Next door is the living room with two angled windows, white sofas, and a fireplace typical of the Dalarna region. The bedrooms are upstairs. Before entering the house, visitors are asked to leave their shoes at the door, so as not to dirty the pale-colored rugs and parquets—a common habit in Sweden.

How could one resist the charm of this legendary region, where, before going to bed on the day of the summer solstice, young women of marriageable age place seven flowers from different fields under their pillows? The boy they dream of that midsummer's night will be their Prince Charming.

In the bedroom, as everywhere in the house, Anneli makes generous use of linen for the sofa and armchair slipcovers, on the bed, and on the table. She also stacks it in her cupboards next to antique white Swedish dishware and some contemporary pieces in black.

As in all Swedish houses, visitors are asked to remove their shoes before entering. A long runner protects the floorboards. Armchairs and table from Anneli's collection.

PREVIOUS SPREAD: *In the living room, a white sofa under the window and, in front, a wooden horse to remind us that we're in Dalarna, whose symbol is the horse. The pair of bookshelves is from Anneli's collection.*

On the first floor, the largest room is devoted to the kitchen and dining area. The three-hundred-year-old pine table comes from a farmhouse. On the floor, the old white pine floorboards are a foot wide and one and a half inches thick—impossible to match with today's materials.

Some of the furnishings come from Anneli's collection (the storage chest, the desk, and the oxblood chairs), others are from the Gustavian era.

On the wall, a
painting by Peter
Claeson, an
important Swedish
artist. The pine desk
with three drawers
has been refinished
and the tabletop
stained black, like
the Gustavian chair,
which is from Anneli's
collection.

In front of most of the windows, one finds these geraniums called mårbackas, *after the name of the manor where the writer Selma Lagerlöf grew them in her garden. They come in only one color, a delicate pale pink that is nearly white, and are found only in Scandinavia.*

The House Under the Olive Trees

The acclaim for Stéphane Olivier has now passed well beyond France, and he is now carrying out work at sites on almost all continents. He has a very formal idea of what a house should be, in which he mixes styles, materials, and periods. He likes the grand, the precious, and the refined as well as the rustic, and he will search to the ends of the earth for the rare object. In Paris, his boutique on the rue de l'Université is a huge curiosity cabinet. There, one finds the unfindable, the never-before-seen, the unexpected; it is a gallery of the extraordinary. Objects and furniture from eighteenth-century France and Sweden sit side by side with carefully curated work by contemporary artists. It is a window onto the far reaches of home decor.

A great traveler, Stéphane had a dream: to be able to forget Paris for just a few moments, to change his universe and escape from the capital to . . . a sheep farm in Provence. But his two boutiques in Paris left him little time to look for one. So when one of his friends offered him a guesthouse at the edge of his property, he did not hesitate for a single moment. It was in fact an old sheepfold built of drystone, clinging to the side of a hill planted with olive trees, with an unparalleled view of the village of Ramatuelle. Renovation had already been completed, the kitchen and bath already installed; all he had to do was show up with his luggage.

The house is bordered along its whole length by an arbored terrace that is protected by a fine metal pergola covered with reed curtains and entwined with jasmine branches. The dining room opens directly onto this terrace through a pair of sculpted doors of Portuguese origin, as does the master bedroom. All meals take place here, sheltered in all seasons from the sun and wind. On the exterior, a stone stairway leads to a stand-alone bedroom, ideal for visiting friends. Naturally, Stéphane has mingled styles: Gustavian with Italian, the provincial with the industrial, the sacred with the exotic. As always with his work, the results are flawless.

Three bronze
Cambodian bowls
mounted on pedestals
pick up the delicate
tones of the collec-
tion of stick insects.
In front of a black
coral, two stuffed
parakeets are perched
on antique wig stands
(Stéphane Olivier
boutique).

On the trellised
terrace, leaning
against a wall loaded
with greenery, an old
carpenter's workbench
serves as a sideboard
with a pair of blown-
glass candle jars and
a terra-cotta grease
pot from Biot. Under
the pergola built by
a local artisan, the
table is dressed with
an antique embroi-
dered tablecloth; the
chairs are Italian,
from the turn of the
century. In a carved
stone tub with iron
bands, three agaves.

Opening onto
the terrace, the
eighteenth-century
carved wooden door
is no doubt of Portu-
guese origin. As a sign
of welcome, Stéphane
has attached a sheet-
metal candleholder
from Savoy.

The eighteenth-century country buffet maintains its original silver-gray patina. The carved wooden donkey comes from an Italian church crèche. A wooden boot tree for cavalry boots makes an unusual base for a lamp.

Behind a daybed upholstered in linen (Caravane), a seventeenth-century shepherd's bench. Across from the fireplace, two wood-working components from the eighteenth century frame the console, an industrial piece from the nineteenth century. Under the eighteenth-century chandelier in beaten iron, instead of a low table, three big stumps of exotic wood. The floor lamp is a piece by Stéphane Olivier.

In front of the linen drapes (Caravane) stands a grotto chair in silver leaf from the eighteenth-century, which was purchased in Italy.

In the bedroom, under an antique botanical chart, the small eighteenth-century bureau comes from Sweden. Near the silvered glass Virgin Mary, two secondhand picture frames decorated with shells have been turned into mirrors. Under a Napoleon III glass bell, a flight of butterflies (Stéphane Olivier boutique).

In the

Shadow

of

Princes

In Paris, a few steps from the Jardin de Luxembourg, and even closer to the Théâtre de l'Odéon, on a street of beautifully unified eighteenth-century architecture, stands a formal building, almost austere but with great elegance, occupying in part the former location of the residence of the princes of Condé. Subtle contrasts reign throughout. As soon as the door opens, the powerful facade gives way to a courtyard full of charm, with its old fountain, its ivy, its ferns, and its camellias, whose blooms light up the end of winter.

"I loved this apartment right away," Florence confides, "probably because of its unusually low ceilings. They give the place such a lovely intimacy while still maintaining a sense of grandeur, in a way similar to some of the private rooms in our châteaux."

The light is gentle, hardly ever direct, and most often reflected by the pale facades of the town houses along the river. Won over by this quiet atmosphere, Florence particularly wanted to avoid any aggressive restoration, subscribing instead to a permanent search for timelessness. She emphasizes the subtle touches that enhance the delicate colors of the antique painted furniture and which lend sparkle to the eighteenth-century textiles that she collects. The classic plan of the apartment suited her perfectly, and she decided to preserve it.

Only the kitchen, which one reaches through a sunroom covered with Virginia creeper, merited some rethinking. In keeping with the studio atmosphere that had attracted her, Florence decided to install two old orangery windows, which separate the sitting area from the work area without interrupting the light and, especially, the feeling of spaciousness. Three black pieces of furniture, arranged in a triangle, elongate the proportions of the room. The walls she had repainted in a shade of gray green that plays off of the foliage of the courtyard and sets off the floor tiles of pink eighteenth-century terra-cotta. Very attentive to the spirit of place, Florence also knows how to create touches of comfort. She has a flair for the art of living in harmony.

Under a Regency mirror in a gilded wooden frame, a Louis XVI bureau, surrounded by eighteenth-century portraits. An arte povera box, a music box, and papier-mâché puppets.

On the shelves in the living room, a clever collection of eighteenth-century objects: Neapolitan crèche figurines, a processional bust of the Virgin, a pair of baroque angels, "master works," an artist's mannequin, and old toys, including a hobbyhorse and a monkey in formal dress on a horse of its own.

In the bathroom, near the 1930s porcelain sink, a panel of painted wood with an oxeye window that offers a glimpse of the next room, and some framed botanical prints.

From floor to ceiling, eighteenth-century tapestry provides sumptuous decoration for the living room. In front of the piano, an unusual Napoleon III chair upholstered in velvet.

The double doors of the living room lead to a bedroom. On one side, a Louis XVI bed with a toile de Jouy bedspread and matching cushions, and a nineteenth-century English officer's rocking chair made of metal; on the other, a table à gibier from Provence under a vanitas. The bust of a child in terra-cotta from the Directoire period, a roof finial in the shape of a bird, a vase made from

a lacemaker's lamp, and an element from an antique gold-leafed railing. Placed on the ground, a puppet's head in a cradle and a small octagonal steeple made of wood.

The moldings and paneling are original. On the eighteenth-century mantelpiece, an artist's mannequin made of wood and leather with a polychrome head, with its hand on a globe. On the Louis XVI armchair, an antique quilt. On the table de vigneron, a number of enameled glass vessels illustrated with images from Grimm's fairy tales, an Italian glass carafe, and a leech bowl.

*By the entryway, a little Provençal secretary,
under a nineteenth-century portrait of a child.*

*Cupboards were
added to the kitchen,
with sliding doors
made of wide slats of
wood painted taupe.
A veranda table and a
painting of parakeets
serve to establish a
garden atmosphere.*

On a wrought-iron easel, a portrait of a child from the Directoire period and a carriage chandelier.

The moldings are the same in the bedroom and living room. In the nook, a nineteenth-century mannequin, and on the armchair, an eighteenth-century indigo kelsch from Alsace. The carousel horse is from the same period.

A simple garden table with slightly distressed black paint serves as a desk. On the wall, a collection of antique drawings.

In the eat-in kitchen, two antique orangery windows separate the dining area from the work area. The stone table with the cast-iron base and the rattan chairs are patio furniture. The floor tile is original.

In a child's bedroom, under the light of a round window, antique toys on a garden pedestal table.

A gorgeous Irish buffet and hutch from the eighteenth century,
made of black-stained wood. It holds antique ceramics, bird-shaped
roof finials, a butcher's emblem, and a stone garden statue.

A White (and Black) *Wedding*

In the 1980s, Fabrice Diomard left Toulouse, abandoning his antique shop, to move to Paris. Since then, he has moved regularly, simply for the pleasure of change and of redeveloping a life within new surroundings. And here is his most recent abode: right in the heart of the Marais, an apartment in a Directoire building, lined with windows looking down onto the rue Saint-Antoine. Farther upstage, the striking facade of the Eglise Saint-Paul—in need of cleaning—dominates with its cupola, and it is hard to take your eyes off the incessant coming and going of the pedestrians who animate the sidewalks of this popular tourist neighborhood. "After the calmness of my house by the Palais-Royal," Fabrice says, "I went from one extreme to the other, but here it is incredibly dynamic and lively."

By virtue of his Scandinavian and Italian origins, this decorator prizes a combination of Gustavian and baroque Italian furnishings. He felt no hesitation about what color to paint the walls: they are white throughout, except in the bedroom, set off from the rest with a dark gray.

"In my previous house," he adds, "I made the same choice, because of the weak light. Here, it's just the opposite—the apartment is bathed in sun—but still, white is my favorite color. I'm all for the mixing of styles, but within a monochrome palette; otherwise it draws attention to the confusion . . . White, and black as well, are in my opinion the best choice to highlight the painted furniture, plaster casts, shells, paintings, and sculptures at the heart of my decor."

This apartment is the antithesis of a fixed museum: the juxtaposition of the antique and the contemporary is honored by the successful marriage of the rigor of Plexiglas and the allure of the furnishings of the past. As proof of his eclecticism, Fabrice has just opened a small gallery on rue Jacob dedicated to his collection of Plexiglas furniture, a happy complement to his antique shop in the Village Suisse in the 15th arrondissement.

PREVIOUS PAGE: *White silk curtains for the window, eighteenth-century candelabra, Directoire armchair, and Le Corbusier chaise longue.*

A collection of plaster casts from a period spanning from the eighteenth to the twentieth century: elements of pillar capitals, bas-reliefs, acanthus leaves, and so on.

Against the backdrop of a black-and-white striped silk curtain, a plaster statue representing Achilles Borghese. The wall sconces are from the 1940s.

*The nineteenth-century ceramic stove is flanked
by two plaster casts placed on a Plexiglas base,
including a dancer by Canova, commissioned
from the artist by Joséphine de Beauharnais.
Plexiglas tables (L'Autre Maison) and an Italian
chandelier from the 1960s customized with
Plexiglas paillettes by Fabrice.*

In front of the black coral, this 1940s obelisk is made of Plexiglas; the three small ones are made of crystal.

On a wall painted matte black, paintings by Fabrice Diomard.

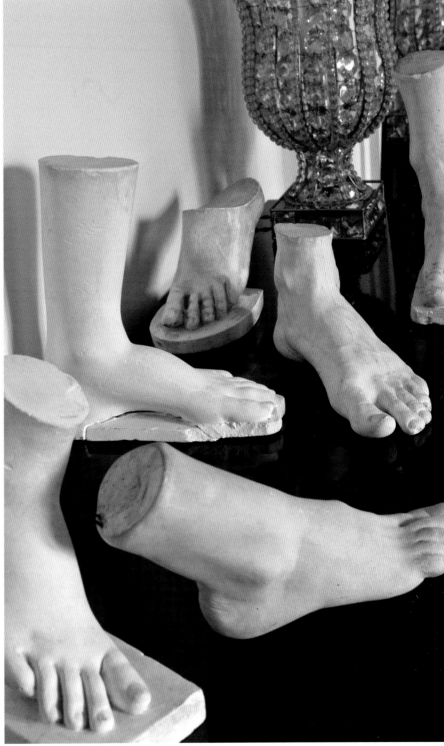

The table, with a surface of alternating black and white stripes, is a creation of Fabrice for L'Autre Maison. Chairs by Verner Panton. Baccarat crystal candlestick; a plaster cast of a Greek bas-relief.

A collection of plaster casts for artists; feet of gladiators and athletes.

Half-hidden by curtains of off-white silk, the Eglise Saint-Paul, not far from the Bastille in Paris, was constructed by Jesuits in the seventeenth century by order of Louis XIII.

A superb Gustavian bench upholstered with hemp, under artwork by Valérie Maffre (L'Autre Maison).

In Search of Times *Past*

Very close to the leisurely Loire, the Pays Baugeois is a country of hills and narrow valleys bristling with twisted steeples and stately houses built of tuffeau stone. The historic capital of the region, proud of its castle built in the fifteenth century by King René, duke of Anjou, the town of Baugé abounds in *hôtels particuliers*, the ornate city mansions built to house royal counselors. There are more than forty hidden along Baugé's tranquil streets, opening onto gardens and flanked with turrets that conceal spiral staircases.

It is in one of these remarkable houses that Frank and Nadège Dolais settled four years ago with their children. These antique dealers left Vannes and their renowned shop on the Place du Marché for the sweet life in Anjou. Their find, neglected for more than twenty years, is one of the most authentic in the city. The main structure dates from 1594. It was expanded and reconfigured over the course of the subsequent centuries. As soon as you walk through the door, you admire the exceptional half-turn staircase, carved from local stone and perfectly restored. Guided by the spirit of the house, they have returned it to its original state. With their own four hands, they scraped the woodwork to uncover the old patina and applied lime plaster with distempers. "To decorate a house is, first of all, to discover its secrets," Frank and Nadège say. "These unknown places, which become familiar with time, whisper their stories to us. It is up to us to know how to listen, so that they may inspire us to find their true soul. We want to live in the present, but surrounded by the past."

At the same time and very close by, they opened their new two-story shop, Quattrocentro. There, they display a beautiful selection of objects, furniture, and paintings that speak to those who truly want to listen.

PREVIOUS PAGE:
In front of the seventeenth-century tuffeau-stone fireplace, on a Spanish gateleg cherry table, a striking pair of swans frames a Spanish reliquary from the seventeenth century. On an eighteenth-century pewter plate, a few turtle shells.

On a black-stained chest of drawers from the Transition period, a collection of Egyptian and Roman heads and busts carved from marble or stone, below an eighteenth-century barometer. The Hungarian point parquet and the Louis XVI of the living room are original, and the mirror is from the Louis XVI period. Near the mantelpiece, a low table constructed out of slabs of slate on a metal base is presided over by an Italian marble bust. The daybed is from the Directoire period; the armchairs are Louis XVI and Regency. On the corner cabinet is a termite's nest.

Under a medallion portrait, a console table from the Regency period and an armillary sphere. On the armchair from the same period, leaning against a leather chest from the eighteenth century, a papier-mâché doll. Over the door, a seventeenth-century knight's helmet of polychrome wood.

PREVIOUS SPREAD: *In front of a screen from Angers, a German carousel horse and a Spanish processional statue; all three are from the eighteenth century. On the rustic Empire pedestal table, various "master pieces" produced by artisans for acceptance in the guild system, including a zinc polyhedron.*

A guest bedroom has been arranged under the rafters and decorated as an artist's studio with watercolor cases, easel, models, sculpture, and so on. An ideal still life serves to inspire visitors' dreams.

Near the window, the small Louis XV table overflows with old manuscripts, along with hourglasses, a spyglass, and a polyhedron. Lined up on the radiator, processional and oratory statuary from the eighteenth century.

The magnificent
tuffeau-stone
staircase, dating
from the seventeenth
century, connects the
two floors.

A series of engravings
on this extraordi-
nary folding screen
recounts the stages of
the life of man, from
birth until death. On
the winter-garden
pedestal table from
the nineteenth century,
a white marble vase is
joined by obelisks and
polyhedrons. Behind
the Swedish chair,
above the fireplace,
a composition of
antique manuscripts.

PREVIOUS SPREAD: *In the huge master bedroom, the bed is from the Louis XVI era. In front of the high window equipped with interior shutters, a black Louis XV table strikes a formal note. On the black marble mantelpiece, a collection of gilded wooden crowns, elements of an altarpiece.*

In the black-and-white bathroom, an artist's pedestal supports a vase filled with seaweed and shells.

Exposed beams and a beautiful tuffeau-stone fireplace for the kitchen, with an eighteenth-century table d'office *that came from a castle in Normandy, a butcher's block from the same period, and a hard stone sink against a slate back-splash. The chairs were milled by a local artisan to match an old design. Suspended in the corner, a dove and a pig's head, the latter an old butcher's insignia.*

Monet's
Gardener

The garden door opens into the universe of Claude Monet, a heavenly landscape of plants and flowers. Thierry Huau is honored with the fine title, among others, of gardener of Giverny. A landscape architect and city planner, he is a specialist in the creation and restructuring of parks and gardens all over the world. An indefatigable traveler, he has worked in Beirut, Hanoi, and Madagascar. Among his accomplishments are creations in New Zealand, Australia, and Saudi Arabia. He has just finished an ambitious project in Angers (Terra Botanica) intended to show off the remarkable diversity of plants and their properties.

Thierry has kept intact his poet and gardener's soul, his ability to marvel at nature, and his childhood memories of hiding bulbs under his bed. Twenty years ago, he bought the former studio of Blanche Hoshedé-Monet, the daughter-in-law of the father of Impressionism, as well as an adorable little pink house on the other side of the courtyard.

The studio is one of the old barns where the monks of the neighboring abbey of Saint-Ouen kept provisions. After restoration and addition work, Thierry moved in.

Around the house, the steeply graded land was entirely wild. He built stairs into the hill to create green rooms, true garden laboratories, not forgetting to add several basins as a nod to the water lilies.

Inside the building, Monet had had a huge fireplace and a large south-facing bay window installed. On the other side, due north, Thierry added a sunroom to protect his exotic plants during the winter. It is bordered by a wall of very old bricks, and completed by a vertical garden. But the true treasure of the house is the library, which, lining the four walls of the living room, contains more than 1,500 books devoted to botany, landscape design, and the environment.

The house seems alive
with the spirit of a
curiosity cabinet: the
rocks, stones, insects,
and fossils of plants
and animals that
form the base of our
knowledge of the
countryside also hold
a place in the belong-
ings of this great
naturalist.

The kitchen looks as
if untouched for a
century, its cupboards
overflowing with
vessels, bottles, jars,
and Thierry's collec-
tion of antique molds.

The dining room opens out onto a little patio; the sparrows come to refresh themselves at a birdbath shaped like a fountain. The metal door and the furniture enhance the feeling of being in an artist's studio.

The study, like the living room, is overwhelmed by books and Thierry's plans for numerous projects.

The living room is located in Monet's former studio. The clever carpenter, Emmanuel Hellot, created the bookshelves out of recycled wooden crates. They have stripped doors, pivoting panels, trompe l'oeil, and a window opening onto the veranda. They contain more than 1,500 works on botany and the art of the garden.

Amélie's Loft

More than half a century ago, this small factory sheltered the large vats of a dyeworks. Abandoned, the place lapsed into profound neglect. In this lamentable state it was then finally put up for sale by its owner. Nevertheless, when Amélie saw the place for the first time, she called to her husband in delight. She hardly saw the corrugated plastic roof packed with asbestos or the cement floor spattered with stains in many colors or the cinder blocks downy with spiderwebs. She only noticed the impressive metal beams of the roof and the structure, the huge footprint, and the industrial feel of the building, which fascinated her. Antoine shared her enthusiasm.

In a few months, they were the new owners of this strange, almost ugly building—with a thousand ideas about how to transform it into a place built to their specifications.

Amélie's architect father-in-law, Bertrand Leclercq, and her antiquarian brother-in-law, Mathieu Leclercq, took part in the restoration, which thus became a family affair. Each took charge of his or her area: Bertrand took care of the arrangement of the interior space; Amélie looked after the colors, which she likes to be bracing, and of the conception for the decor; and Mathieu, who had opened the nearby Espace Nord-Ouest, a group of antique sellers all working in the same register, assumed the charge to find salvaged factory furnishings, which he combined with various elements from the eighteenth and nineteenth centuries.

Two years later, Antoine and Amélie see only the advantages of life here: above all, of a home with a living space of more than 1,000 square feet. Adult life is organized around this central area, with the master bedroom near the bathroom, the kitchen, the study, and the television room. On the second floor, a catwalk leads to children's bedrooms and a playroom. Other assets: the light that streams in through the huge windows and, finally, the pleasure of living in a house unlike any other.

Aided by architect and antiquarian relatives, Antoine and Amélie were intent on preserving the spirit of the building's origins in every detail. The guardrail is made out of steel tubing. Above are metal beams which, in the master bedroom, go with the lockers in the dressing room. Here and there, a few touches of red lacquer punctuate the space, which is otherwise fitted out in monochromatic gray and black.

In perfect accord with the industrial spirit, this extremely modern gas fireplace operates by remote control. The bergère and the deer-antler-and-drop-bead chandelier were picked up at Espace Nord-Ouest in Bondues.

Closet doors of
stripped wood
contrast with the
modern refrigerator.
The raspberry red
central island is lit
by a factory suspen-
sion lamp from
a warehouse in
Tourcoing.

A last touch of red in the kitchen comes from a poppy decal. The suspension lamp and the industrial metal cabinet with twelve drawers, whose cover opens as a chest, are both salvage pieces.

FOLLOWING SPREAD: *In front of a monumental rolling door dating from the construction of the factory and under a grand crystal chandelier, the dining room table is made of simple planks of scaffolding mounted on four wheels. On the sideboard, whose wooden surface has been recovered in zinc and placed on a metal base, sit a model boat and a painting by Youri Leroux. To add movement to this large wall without an opening, a zinc dormer window placed on the ground serves as the frame for a mirror.*

In the Light of the Atelier

A lover of the countryside of Normandy as much as the light of Provence, the painter Camille Hilaire translated both into bright colors in his work. In the 1960s, to get away from the capital, he moved to the center of a village in the Vexin. When the farmhouse opposite his home came up for sale, he bought it in order to install a large studio space there. Since then, his daughter Pascale has reorganized this second house as a home.

The exposed stone walls of the house disappear behind a climbing vine, and the alley that runs along it is paved with reconstituted stones, perfectly aged. In the garden, Pascale has added various relaxing corners. Here, an old stone bench where the ivy likes to climb; there, under a gloriette, a table and a few seats on which to bask on a summer afternoon. Formerly a secondary studio for her father, the central room makes use of all the space under the rafters. It has been painted pale gray to reflect the maximum amount of light and to set off the works of the master. Pascale has installed the dining room there, and has created all around the table various charming nooks, accumulating collections of objects from the eighteenth and nineteenth centuries, which she has organized by affinity, color, and style. She has thus followed the same rules of elegance for the garden and the house to create a subtle atmosphere, dedicated to harmony and the past. Pascale has a passion for antiques and interior design. She has opened a shop in La Roche-Guyon, right by the castle, where she stages beautiful scenes in a small house arranged as if she lived there. With old store cases or notary bookshelves filled with plaster and stone busts, stuffed game animals, pastel paintings, and oils on canvas, it is a voyage outside of time.

In the kitchen, the cabinets, the bistro table, its wooden tabletop, and the chairs from Burgundy are all painted a soft celadon green inspired by the paintings of Camille Hilaire. On the counter, a collection of candy jars are elegantly displayed. Under an ancestor's portrait from the eighteenth century, the bed is covered with a needlepointed quilt; the little bedside table has been refinished. The wooden bookshelves were built by the owner himself. The stepladder was bought years ago from the Manufrance catalog. On the top shelf, a collection of papier-mâché horses, children's toys from the nineteenth and twentieth centuries.

Here, too, Pascale has chosen the colors of the velvet of the couch as a reference to the colors in her father's paintings.

Near the window, a group of carousel horses and
children's toys. Near the bookshelf, a lyre-backed
chair in front of a small Louis XV desk. On top,
Pascale has placed a Louis-Philippe writing case,
which was in the family, and a miniature by
Paul Jance.

On the rustic oak Louis XV buffet, a lantern, a
mirror from Burgundy, a glass carafe with a
pewter band, a Spanish Virgin Mary from the
nineteenth century, and a spike candlestick of
turned wood from the Périgord. On the dummy,
an embroidered vest from the eighteenth century.

PREVIOUS SPREAD: *On the table, an embroidered quilt and faience dishes, a Louis XVI design from H.B. Choisy-le-Roi (Plaisir d'Antan). In front of the window, the console table overflowing with knickknacks is a bistro table resurfaced with zinc.*

Near the front door, a veritable bestiary, with an English diorama on the wall: a pheasant, a weasel, a jay, a kingfisher. On the rustic table, which has been repainted, a Paul Jance miniature and some taxidermy animals: two coots, a duckling, and so on. On the wall, two collections of butterflies.

On the windowsill, a cider carafe and some engraved glasses.

In homage to her great-grandfather, Paul Jance, Pascale has placed before his portrait, painted by a friend, the piano stool that her father sat on to paint. On the chair, near the Medici vase filled with seashells, a stuffed barn owl.

Patrimony

Revisited

In 1733, a rich farmer from the Lille region decided to have a huge residence constructed to house his kin. But before the work was finished, the man departed for the next world. It was thus decided, in view of the enormous size of the building, to transform it into two twin houses, one for each of his sons. The brick facade, accented with stones from Lezennes, is typical of the period and region. Recorded in the *Patrimoine des Communes du Nord*, it is one of the oldest houses in the center of a city of ten thousand inhabitants, a few minutes outside of Lille.

In the 1980s, the owners asked the architect Bertrand Leclercq to help them rehabilitate it. What he didn't know was that the house he was working on would one day belong to his son. In 2006, Mathieu Leclercq established his home there. "Life is paradise here," he says. "The market is seconds away, on the little plaza planted with trees—the school, too. You can do everything on foot. You have the impression of being self-sufficient within a very small universe." At the advice of his architect father and designer mother, Mathieu started his career training at an auction house. Thus was born his passion for antique furniture. Very soon, he took his first steps as an antique dealer in Montpellier. Some time later, he returned to his home turf and opened a shop in Marcq-en-Baroeul with two friends.

Years passed. Some friends who dealt in antiques and secondhand goods, specializing equally in the eighteenth and nineteenth centuries, salvage and contemporary style, proposed that he join them in a large center for antiques that they were organizing under the glass warehouse roof of an old wallpaper factory in Bondues. Mathieu and his associates decided to follow them into this enterprise, which was as audacious as it was seductive. Thus was created Espace Nord-Ouest, where a group of eighteen partners, most of whom grew up together, work with shared enthusiasm—and equal success.

This terra-cotta Venus from nineteenth-century Italy is a copy of the one in The Hall of Mirrors at Versailles. The teak armchair is a reproduction of one from a transatlantic ocean liner. Under the rafters, a bedroom loft has been built, accessible via ladder. The small dresser, stripped of its mahogany veneer, has been painted oxblood red. At the end of the bed, a grisaille painting and a carved wooden cherub.

The dining room table is an industrial machine base. The dishes are slipware from Dieulefit.

To add style to the bathroom, the mirror has been replaced by a seascape, and the wall tile has been hidden behind shutters.

To close off the shelves, Mathieu employed a set of stripped wooden shutters. Over the pine mantelpiece enhanced by a Louis XVI trumeau mirror, trophies made of régule (a zinc alloy).

On an eighteenth-century dresser from eastern France, which has maintained its original red patina, the griffon is Italian terra-cotta. The Medici vase stands on a nineteenth-century cast-iron pedestal table next to another, signed by Grassin, from the manufacturer in Arras.

The fireplace of local bricks was built according to a design by Bernard Leclercq. On the right, against a Louis XV panel, Mathieu has placed a mirror from the same period. On the Regency chest of drawers built of regional elm, an allegorical sculpture of water, in eighteenth-century terracotta (Espace Nord-Ouest). The chandelier is a reproduction from the 1950s. Against the back of the sofa, a butcher's table lit by a nineteenth-century cast-iron Cupid wired as a lamp. Fixed to the wall, an oak caryatid from the Louis XIV era and, on the column, an eighteenth-century terracotta statue from the south of France.

Near the refinished nineteenth-century china cabinet, a Gustavian clock and a factory table of oak and pine. Near the door, another eighteenth-century terra-cotta statue. The low table is a 1940s game table from a bistro, whose legs have been cut down and whose surface has been covered with zinc.

As Time Goes By

*B*ob and Chantal Maderou have always been keen on antiques and home decor, to the point of having devoted their best years and all their talents to the cause. Today, in a house that has evolved according to the rhythms of their passions—their occasionally sudden desire to change everything, and their need to create extraordinary tableaux—they have stood back and turned the page, choosing a life that is calmer, less crazy, and also sweeter and more domestic. It is a deliberate move that they have not regretted—but rather the contrary. After all, don't they live near Paris in a dream house that, after so many years of antiquing and various inspirations, has attained perfection? Everywhere the eye rests is touched by imagination and poetry.

Chantal has a sense of grandeur. She is often inspired by the theater, borrowing various elements from it on which she plays with humor. She loves the oversize, the profuse, the multiple. She also loves to make things herself—for example the giant nests formed from garden umbrellas over which she has trained creeping vines. An admirer of Axel Vervoordt and Walda Pairon, she likes to go on trips to Belgium or to Scandinavian countries, where she appreciates the cult of simplicity, the purity, the chic beauty. Her imagination is a perpetual motor in quest for new ideas, which she immediately puts into practice at home.

Bob, meanwhile, keeps up in his own way. Several dozen years ago, he built the greenhouse that extends the house so agreeably into the garden with his own hands. Today, that is the room where they most love to live, protected from exterior noise but bathed in sunlight. While he was at it, he also put in a little orangery in parallel which serves as a study. At the back of the garden, he installed two little wooden houses as toolsheds. They quickly became the preserve of their grandchildren instead. Those children are now grown, but Chantal has transformed the sheds into bedrooms for their exclusive use.

Three hunting trophies in a child's bedroom above a Directoire bed and walls covered in white wainscoting. Four antique doors on the living room bookshelves. The two center ones have wire-net doors, allowing a glimpse of a superb collection of antique pottery on the top half and contemporary pottery on the bottom (by Anna Tópolincka-Bordyne), united by the same color hue. Face to face, on a Regency chest of drawers and a butcher's table, two pairs of Guatemalan balustrade lamps (Marie-Claude Orsini). In front of the window, under the orchids, three small alabaster statues.

Between two windows, the shelves are loaded with old books bound in leather. On the Louis XVI console table, in a Medici vase, a bunch of deer antlers.

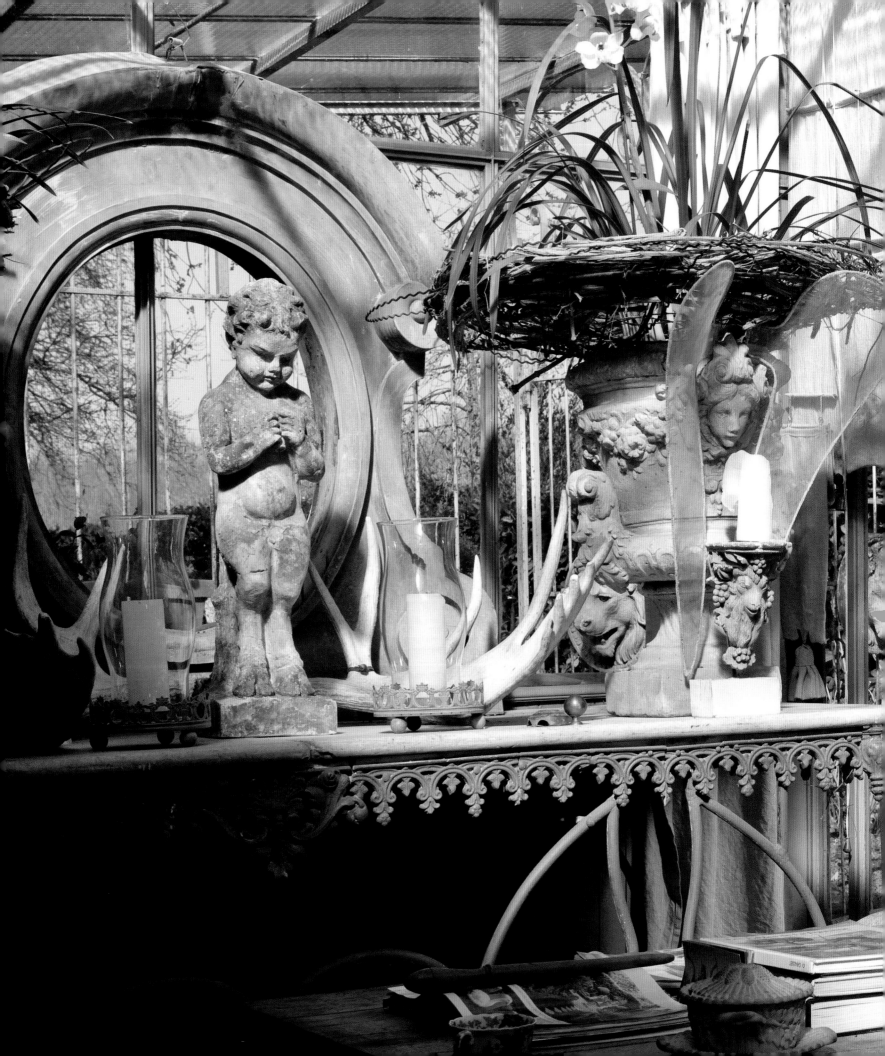

PREVIOUS SPREAD: *The charm of the veranda makes it the vital center of the house, and Chantal expresses all her talent there with a still life on a* table à gibier: *a stone garden statue and vase crowned with a giant nest woven out of ivy and brimming with orchids, next to an oxeye window and some deer antlers.*

Across from the veranda, Bob's orangery.

Neck swathed in linen, a doe's head is mounted on the window frame, above a stone sink equipped with a brass swan's head faucet.

Pottery by Anna Tópolincka-Bordyne.

*In the orangery, a cabinet with a reworked Louis XVI
facade, and, near the pedestal table, an armchair of
cement "branches." Iron wire chandelier with drop
crystals (Valérie Kling). On the column, a cement basin.*

PREVIOUS SPREAD: *The kitchen, with a* table en cabaret, *to which has been added a slate tabletop, surrounded by four chairs of the Directoire period. The Delft-style faience tiles are protected by two cast-iron firebacks. One comes from Savoy, the other from Provence. The wooden pediment is a detail from a hunting buffet. The confectionery jars were purchased in Belgium.*

On the living room mantelpiece, bouquets of glass beads fixed on iron wire (Valérie Kling) in Medici vases. The console table, made from two newel posts united by a sheet of marble, sits under an eighteenth-century frame, which outlines a mirror from the same period. The coffee table is made from the surface of a brickmaker's table, attached to an X-shaped truss base. Above the nineteenth-century sofa, a remarkable large mirror mounted in a frame ornamented with twining branches.

Under two glass bells placed on the buffet table, two sugarloaves.

The *Eighteenth Century* Suits Her So Well

When the owner of this apartment in the 10th arrondissement of Paris asked her to come and restore it, the decorator Laure du Chatenet did not know what awaited her on this narrow street, at the end of a slender corridor and up a steep, dark staircase. She was completely surprised to discover a huge and incredibly bright space at the top. The apartment is set astride two separate buildings. The first, facing the street, was built in the eighteenth century and then enlarged in the nineteenth, when a factory was constructed within the interior courtyard. This creates two very distinct spaces: one with a relatively low ceiling that provides an intimate atmosphere, the other with the proportions of a loft, with a wall and a roof made of glass, framed by a terrace. It is this contrast that gives the place its appeal.

For the construction, the owner gave Laure carte blanche. A die-hard fan of eighteenth-century style, she selected for the colors a harmonious assortment of oatmeals and grays, subtle tones that disappear behind the furniture and decorative objects. The floating parquet floor of cherrywood, which added little interest, was replaced by wide planks of antique oak. Laure made a tour of her favorite shops and collected a mix of eighteenth- and nineteenth-century pieces and modern furniture, intended to give the space the relaxed look she appreciates. And she added numerous objects from her own collection. In effect, she became far more than a decorator. With this unusual composite apartment, Laure has found the ideal setting for a successful marriage of modern furnishings and wood with the patina of age.

In 2004, she started her own company, Maison Caumont, a name that refers to a family home she particularly loved. Beyond a line of furniture, she has imagined a collection of art objects, trumeau mirrors, lamps, linens, and paper goods, all inspired by wallpapers and documents from the eighteenth century, reworked and set off by more modern prints. Everything is made artisanally in France.

PREVIOUS PAGE:
From the landing, you reach the living room on one side, and can continue up the stairs to the terrace. Under a painting inherited through the family, a rolling studio table, found at the Paul-Bert flea market. On top, pitchers, a vase, and dishes (Regards) and a pair of lamps with decorated lamp shades (Maison Caumont).

The metal desk with drawers comes from a post office, and the swivel chair from the 1950s was bought secondhand. Floor lamp by Fly.

Above the bed, a piece of a gilded wooden pediment, and on each side, serving as nightstands, a pair of small Louis XVI console tables, also of gilded wood, with two lamps (Maison Caumont).

Across from the Le Corbusier chaise longue, a provincial buffet from the eighteenth century. On the wall, near a Louis XVI armchair, a series of engravings on the theme of travel, created by Laure from old documents, as was the lamp shade ornamented with an engraving.

The kitchen is located under the terrace. The low cabinets were already present; a professional countertop work surface from a restaurant has been added, along with a small high-end stove (La Cornue).

On the mantel, a couple of characters made of Thiry ceramic, and, on each side of the antique mirror, a pair of engravings on the theme of butterflies.

A piece of furniture built for mail sorting at a post office makes a perfect desk. On the wall, a series of "curiosity" engravings, a creation of Laure (Maison Caumont), as are the paper goods and the small printed lamps.

In the bathroom, a
Louis XVI chair
maintains the atmo-
sphere. There is
no risk of exposure
here, so the reproduc-
tion bathtub (Jacob
Delafon) has been
installed in front of
the window. On the
rolling metal table,
which comes from
a printing press, a
tailor's dummy. The
wall on the left is
waxed concrete; the
floor and the wall on
the right are covered
in cement tiles.

A *Family* Antique Shop

 An hour from Paris, the little village of Condé-sur-Vesgre, unchanged for decades, centers on a tree-lined church square. It truly looks like a postcard. Edith Piaf had a house nearby. The inhabitants of Condé are proud of the church, and people come from miles away to stand under under the astonishing framework shaped like a boat's hull and admire the sixteenth-century windows, which have been recognized as historical monuments by the state. Those alone are worth the trip. However, along the edge of this square is a small seventeenth-century building of three stories, which once housed the communal oven. Originally the stories were connected only via an exterior stairway. In the ensuing century, the top floor remained an attic accessible by ladder, but the two others, destined to become a residence, were linked by an interior stair.

A tenant there for several years, Colette Jacoillot became a little more attached to the house each day. She felt deeply rooted there. She started operating a store on the first floor along with her daughter Sarah, who, like her, was a dealer of antiques—they have a stall at the flea market in Saint-Ouen and exhibit together at various fairs.

One day, she decided to go to the landlord and see if she could convince him to sell her the building on good terms. The business was quickly concluded, and the new owner found herself on cloud nine, for she had loved this old house as her own for many years. Now free to transform it, she decided to preserve its authentic character and not modify the layout but keep the patchwork of little spaces, giving a function to each. The third floor, still only an attic, was quickly linked to the second with its own stairway, and a large greenhouse, built by an artisanal ironworker, was added on the garden side.

The meadow behind the house had been a bit neglected. Today, it has been reworked with taste and antiques, and slopes down, here and there, into charming little corners with stripped wood shutters covered with ivy, garden bells, long deck chairs, and other furnishings from last century.

PREVIOUS PAGE:
On the pine buffet refinished by Colette, a small ebony curiosity cabinet inlaid with ivory, the head of a carousel horse, and an Iranian vase lamp. Above, a nineteenth-century oil painting.

A dominant element in the kitchen is The Bec Salé in the Storm, *an oil on canvas from the nineteenth century placed over the table. The rustic chairs are English, and the pine hutch is from Savoy.*

The wooden buffet has been refinished. On a piece of wooden paneling, Colette has attached a vase and some ornamental carved wooden fragments: palm leaves, an ear of wheat, and so on. The lamp is made out of a wooden baluster. Near the puppet's head, the sandstone pot is typically Alsatian.

PREVIOUS SPREAD: *The stones that make up the fireplace came from a salvager; they were previously the lintel and two columns around a window. A nineteenth-century trumeau mirror adds height. Near sofas covered in antique hemp sheets, a pair of Louis XVI-style bergères. On the pine buffet, refinished in-house, an Iranian vase lamp.*

Near the spike-candlestick lamp, the model is a replica of a house in the Parc de Saint-Cloud.

The walnut library stair is decorative. On it is the head of a warthog and a Scottish wooden model of a waiter. Above a swan from a carousel, a pair of carved wooden angel wings.

The walls, covered with wide wooden battens that
have been lightly sanded and then whitewashed,
give the room a Gustavian feel.

Above a winter-garden console table with a marble
top, an eighteenth-century barometer and a
wooden model of an English manor house. The
chest of drawers, made of black-stained wood
incrusted with mother-of-pearl, is from Syria.

Deep in the Creuse, a *Forgotten* Farmhouse

The stonemasons of the Creuse have been celebrated since the end of the Middle Ages for their knowledge and skill. The poverty of this region and the rigors of its climate obliged farmers to supplement their meager revenues with additional work at the end of the harvest. Leaving the women and children to look after the livestock, they set themselves to learning the trades of stonecutting, paving, plastering, roofing, and sometimes even architecture. They turned up at all the great cathedral building sites, even as far away as Uppsala in Sweden. They also participated in the construction of the seawalls at La Rochelle, the château at Versailles, and, in Paris, the apartment buildings of the Haussmann era. It is hardly surprising then that their houses attract those who love beautiful construction, especially given that the region boasts an unmatched tranquility. The lack of transportation keeps the Creuse off the beaten path, out of reach of the great tourist migrations.

This is one of those true local farmhouses, dating from the seventeenth century and passed down through inheritance to its current owners, descendants of an old local family. Built in the shadow of a church, it sat uninhabited for twenty years, as if forgotten. A painter who lived in the village once took it as a studio, but it remained in its raw state.

Sensitive to its authentic character, the new arrivals strived to preserve this feeling without sacrificing comfort. Naturally, they turned to the region to find the artisans—a painter, a mason, a woodworker—who, by their excellent work, confirmed the reputation of their ancestors. Before the renovation, only two rooms on the first floor were habitable: those where the farmers had once lived. The rest—a sheepfold, huge granaries where feed was stored, and several rooms that still had dirt floors—offered great opportunities for expansion.

Today, it is a true family house, serenely awaiting the arrival of new Creusois generations.

All the elements that form the personality of the farmhouse have been maintained: its beams, its old oak doors with their latches, the flagstone-patterned cement floor, and the exposed stone walls—except on the exterior walls, for better insulation, since the winters are often harsh. The living room paneling was added in the nine-teenth century.

PREVIOUS SPREAD:
*The huge fireplace
built of local granite
includes a bread oven
and niches where food
was kept warm. The
sink, also granite,
serves as a nook for
wolves carved out of
birch and mushrooms
made of plaster or
found in the woods.
A sheep, old tools,
wooden shoes. And,
amid this slightly
somber atmosphere, a
few touches of white
lend softness and
light: the floor and
table lamps, the white
linen slipcovers for the
chairs, the hemp cloth
for the table. In front
of the high window,
a group of antique
carafes and jars.*

Small, charming details: an antique jar and a few packets of envelopes tied with string. An iron bowl with birds and a collection of second-hand wicker baskets next to a vase of wildflowers.

The burlap lamp shade has been whitened with acrylic paint. The wood lace flowerpot full of candles comes from an antique shop in the Creuse, as do the wooden horse-drawn carriages, children's toys placed on a painter's table. A collection of bottles on a small black-stained wooden shelf.

Like a canopy over a four-poster bed, the mansard roof makes the bedroom feel more intimate. A portrait of a little girl, whose blue dress served as inspiration for the color of the walls. Bobbin lamps (Blanc d'Ivoire) and duvet (IKEA).

Under the slope of the stairs, a Regency bureau, some small paintings, and chromos from the nineteenth century. The terra-cotta lamp was painted, and the lamp shade covered in burlap.

On the landing of the stair leading to the bedrooms, a small metal table de toilette *from the nineteenth century and a pair of doll wardrobes, antiques found in the region and hung on the wall.*

Above the dresser
(IKEA), a torn piece
of an old drawing
has been glued onto
an antique manu-
script. In the stairwell,
photos of the village
from the 1900s
have been digitized,
enlarged, and framed.
Bowl by
Astier de Villatte.

*Grape harvesters'
table for meals in
the corner of the
living room. In two
suspended barrel
hoops, a stuffed
woodcock. Framed
on the wall, charts
of the coats of arms
for a jeweler, bought
secondhand at the
Bastille fair.*

An
Attic
in
Stockholm

The roofs of Stockholm are black, but under the astonishing vault of one, Martine Colliander's loft is entirely white. A designer who loves antique linens, and the creator of the "White Sense" collection sold in Europe and the United States, she bears a separate passion for the Gustavian furnishings of her country and draws design inspiration from eighteenth-century models for her collection of furniture, finished in the old style, which she produces as well. At the same time, she has just opened her new shop in Stockholm, Le Testament Français, where she sells furniture and objects from the eighteenth and nineteenth centuries, collected for the most part in France. An enthusiast of the natural look, of the authentic and evocative, she has renovated a *torkvind* in the center of the city, a huge attic space once used by the inhabitants to dry their laundry. Wisely, she kept the original structure and simply cleaned or bleached, where it was not salvageable, the terra-cotta tile floor. Another original touch: the chimneys of the other apartments converge at a central point, an imposing masonry flue in the form of a pyramid of terraced bricks. Martine has whitewashed them. This architectural element climbing toward the roof, which still maintains its original function, gives the room its soul.

Each section of the apartment is organized in small spaces around this pyramid: the kitchen, followed by the dining room, then the living room, and finally the study, under the peak of the roof. But to the mistress of the house, the best room of all, her private paradise, has only the sky for a roof: it is the terrace with a vast view out over the city and crammed with white flowers of all kinds. There she passes the endless summer evenings, under a sun that never disappears over the horizon. Flowers are found in abundance inside the apartment as well, especially geraniums, those *mårbackas* of an incomparably pale hue, which climb in dainty arabesques.

In sum, it is a timeless decor, with a subtle "Swedish-style" harmony that fills this place with a rare sweetness.

Through the book-shelves, an antique double door of stripped pine leads to a guest bedroom. To the side, the little terrace that looks out over the black roofs of Stockholm is Martine's favorite place. Throughout the apartment, she has carefully preserved the original terra-cotta tile floor.

PREVIOUS SPREAD: *All the chimneys in the apartment building converge at a central point in the attic: a huge ventilation flue built out of bricks arranged in tiers, which is responsible for much of the allure of this unusual home. It divides the space into two areas: the study, with a long worktable simply covered with a sheet of linen, and the dining room area. On the glass doors of the hutch, Martine has pasted old wallpaper with a pattern of leaves.*

White dominates in the furnishings as well as on the walls, in the materials as in the art objects. From one style to another, this provides harmony and generates that refined, monochrome universe that Martine so enjoys recreating in her various decoration workshops in Paris as in Stockholm. The high window in the stairwell is veiled with a finely embroidered antique curtain, allowing a glimpse of the delicate mårbackas.

PREVIOUS SPREAD:
The back of the attic is closed off by a huge set of shelves that extends up to the rafters and constitutes a key aspect of the decor. Books on the top shelves can be reached by means of a rough ladder. All elements of the furnishings (chairs, hutch, and armchairs) are from Martine Colliander's collection.

The intimacy of the bedroom is protected by a monogrammed organdy veil from Martine's "White Sense" collection. On the floor, a tufted cotton rug adds a comfortable touch.

Although the dining room chairs are reproductions from her collection, this is a real Gustavian one from the eighteenth century.

The kitchen is outfitted in small, salvaged furnishings, all painted white. On the shelves, Martine has placed faience dishes, also white, some of which are from France.

The House that *Wanted* a Garden

*B*ecause Xavier and Tiphaine had lived in the fast lane for years, they wanted a house full of charm, softness, and light. A peaceful house, preferably in a city not far from Paris so as not to be too far away from their families. "We were looking for a big house," Xavier recounts, "with private space for each of our two boys. Like all the eighteenth-century *hotels particuliers*, this one had serious assets—high ceilings, a majestic staircase, big windows with wooden interior shutters, stone fireplaces with mirrors above them. All these details, along with a garden that was neither too big nor too small, won us over."

The layout of the house was satisfactory except for a few details: The bathrooms were cramped, and so it made sense to recoup some space from the too-numerous bedrooms to create suites with dressing rooms, since the new owners having a yearning for comfort. The kitchen, as well, had to be completely reconceived.

They entrusted the work to Stéphanie Vérilhac, a decorator whose work they had admired at the house of some friends. She is also a designer with her own line of products (paper goods, textiles) for children.

"You have carte blanche," Tiphaine told her. "Act as if the house was yours. One single request: bring us as close as possible to nature. Bring the trees into the house!" Stéphanie began by rearranging the second floor, where she put in a huge bow window. The spot lent itself to the addition because a terrace already existed there, with a pretty flight of stairs descending to the garden. It was this excellent idea that gave the house its cheerful atmosphere and cool, bright feel. The floorboards and tiles were in fine shape; only the outdated paint job had to be redone. Finally, it was time to furnish the house, Xavier and Tiphaine having kept almost nothing from their previous apartment.

A tireless antiquer, Stéphanie finds it a pleasure to search for, buy, and store objects in her garage, then transform them. She has a thousand ideas a second. When a piece attracts her eye, her imagination goes to work about how to make the most of it, how to transform it, and where to place it to set it off to best advantage. The album of her creations is a thick one. "It's a little like acrobatics, but I love it," she says. And so do her clients, it seems.

In the sunroom, a glass confectioner's shelf displays antique jars and candy dishes. Over the marble butcher's table, the wall sconce is a wrought-iron coat hook from Marrakech, on which a glass bell has been hung. The doorway that leads to the library is set off by an eighteenth-century garden gate that has accompanied the owners throughout their moves.

In the living room, the fireplace is framed by a pair of refinished buffets in the Louis XVI style. They were salvaged at the time the house was purchased. Near a mother and child scene, the work of the painter Capronnier, the Napoleon III dummy on its copper stand was bought in Belgium. Under the glass bell, the bust is a nineteenth-century copy of Houdon. On the wall, a nineteenth-century herbarium; the large American chaise longue is from Crate and Barrel.

Flour, tea cookies, and apples fill a beautiful collection of confectionery jars and candy dishes lined up on the console table in the dining room.

The living room opens onto the sunroom through a double-glassed door which, before the expansion, led out directly onto the garden. On the buffet, near a collection of antique ankle boots, a church niche holds a mannequin found in the street.

Stéphanie transformed this old-fashioned armoire found at an antiques fair into a bathroom fixture, with a basin set into a surface of waxed cement, above a small storage cupboard. The depth of the armoire has been modified.

The shower-bath has been tiled using the tadelakt method with cabochons of mother-of-pearl. The walls are finished with storm-gray tadelakt plaster. A mirrored oxeye adds depth. A shower drain, made to measure by Volevatch, can be stoppered for a luxurious pool-like bathing space.

A boudoir precedes the bathroom. On the gray marble mantelpiece, a pair of vase lamps. In front of the window, near the chaise longue, a church spike candlestick.

In the guest bedroom, the canopy was created with a pediment from an armoire and its box beam, to which have been attached a pair of velvet curtains lined with gabardine and a crystal chandelier to amplify the theatrical effect. The thickness of the wall has permitted the insertion of an old glass case from a department store, which displays apothecary jars and antique perfume bottles.

*Stéphanie ordered these pieces to measure at
L'Antiquaire du Fourneau, in the Saint-Étienne
region, where one can design a high-end range
using antique components. They include two
ovens, a plate warmer, a large induction cooker,
and a grill.*

In the summer dining area, Stéphanie found a large haberdasher's chest that had been appropriated as a candy counter. With a few department-store shelves added, the piece became a hutch and buffet. She filled it with glassware of all kinds: jars, candy dishes, bowls, decanters, and so on.

Au Temps des

Cerises

In the Maisons-Laffitte park, the Stable of the Bronze Horse is a legendary place that saw many hours of glory over the last century. Then it was left abandoned, squatted in, and even vandalized. The buildings are impressive: two English-style pavilions framing a majestic entry gate and, at the back of a huge courtyard, stables, stalls for the horses, saddleries occupying long buildings with yellow ocher walls, not to mention a pretty little house for the stable hands. This exceptional estate seemed fairly out of reach for a private individual. It took Philippe Alric and Sophie Lambert to imagine moving there one day and to transform that dream into reality. He, a show rider and riding instructor, dreamed of creating his own stable. She, an antiques dealer and the proprietor of a shop, Au Temps des Cerises in Saint-Germain-en-Laye, was looking for a beautiful spot to stage the antiques sales that she holds regularly. She could find no better frame for the eighteenth-century and Gustavian pieces that she hunts for all year. The project required the will to move mountains and to survive all the tribulations of managing such a property. It took ten hellish years to realize their vision.

Relying on period photographs, they were determined to find the materials and the original colors in order to restore the house and the stables. In the house, the interior walls were knocked down, the beaten-earth floor was covered with salvaged floor tile, and woodwork, antique doors, and a fireplace of Touraine stone lent their charm to the rooms. Sometime later, after acquiring three superb orangery doors, they decided to build an extension onto the house. This room, oriented due south, is today a living room bathed in light, embraced by the garden from end to end.

Paint colors inspired by Scandinavian houses, furniture finished in monochromatic gray, and stripped wood mingle their soft tones to create the Franco-Swedish atmosphere so dear to Sophie's heart.

ABOVE LEFT AND FOLLOWING SPREADS: *The living room, with Sophie's three orangery doors, has great allure. These doors played a decisive role in the choice to expand the house. The centerpiece of the room is the Louis XVI fireplace, with two sofas draped in linen and a Louis XV banquette. The coffee table, made of simple raw planks on a pair of trestles, contrasts with the Aubusson-style rug. The eighteenth-century bookshelves were painted, and a fine hemp fabric in a faded color masks their interior. Suspended from the whitewashed beams, an Italian chandelier (Au Temps des Cerises).*

In Sophie's bedroom,
a trumeau mirror
at the head of the
bed, two balusters
mounted as lamps,
two Louis XV bergères,
a miniature step-
ladder filled with
books, and a pair of
shutters placed on the
ground in the corner.

Two steps with oak
treads lead to the
living room. Between
the two stripped
wooden doors, which
still have their
original hardware, a
verdure tapestry and
a curved Swedish
chest of drawers made
out of pine (Au Temps
des Cerises).

PREVIOUS SPREAD:
In a style that takes us back two centuries, the finishes on the period furniture, which come from Sophie's boutique, are distressed as though worn by time. The Gustavian table is Swedish, as is the Mora clock, the characteristic chairs, the eighteenth-century two-story buffet, and the chandelier with drop crystals. A fragment of carved woodwork accents the doorway, which leads into the living room full of a subtle harmony of various whites.

Thanks to the whitened floors and the whitewashed beams and walls, soft light filters throughout the house, even into this corridor serving the bedrooms. Sophie has aimed for symmetry, with a pair of console tables over which are two Swedish wooden panels, paintings on wood, two terra-cotta pine-cone finials, and a pair of Louis XVI wall sconces.

For Violette's bedroom, a Directoire bed under two hanging lamps decorated by Sophie. A rustic ladder serves as a clothes rack.

With its oxeye, its funny little suspension lamps, and its sheet-metal wall lamps, whose gray tone is picked up by the curtains under the counter, the kitchen maintains an old-fashioned charm. The stove is by La Cornue; the countertop and backsplash are salvaged tile, as is the floor. All the accessories were bought secondhand, even the drying rack.

The kitchen opens onto the garden through a double door. Also from salvage are the doors of the kitchen cabinets, made from old château shutters, and the door, which has been fitted not with glass but with metal netting. The table is Dutch and the chair Scandinavian.

Address Book

Page 6

Aurélien and Pascale Deleuze
La Maison Noble de Bugnein
Phone 00 33 (0) 6 86 84 93 18
www.magiedeslieux.com
www.uneameenplus.com

Page 20

Boutique Oscar and Clothilde
Styrmansgatan 10/12
11454 Stockholm, Sweden
Phone 00 46 (0) 8 611 53 00
www.oscarclothilde.com
alexander@oscarclothilde.com

Page 34

Sophie Prételat
Boutique Anges et Démons
2 bis, rue Jehanne d'Arc
49730 Montsoreau, France
Phone 00 33 (0) 2 41 38 71 82
00 33 (0) 6 03 56 09 26

Page 44

marlene.cassiers@numericable.fr
Phone 00 33 (0) 6 26 56 58 00

Page 58

Dominique Pol
Phone 00 33 (0) 6 07 95 09 52

Page 76

Société Coquecigrues
Phone 00 33 (0) 2 37 82 64 14
www.coquecigrues.com
coquecigrues@libertysurf.fr

Page 96

Garbo
Brahegatan
211437 Stockholm, Sweden
Phone 00 46 (0) 8 661 60 08
www.garbointeriors.com
carin_carl@hotmail.com

Page 108

Boutique Stéphane Olivier
3, rue de l'Université
75007 Paris, France
Phone 00 33 (0) 1 42 96 10 00
rivegauche@stephaneolivier.fr

La Petite Maison
10, rue Paul Bert
93400 Saint-Ouen, France
Phone 00 33 0 (1) 40 10 56 69

Page 132

Boutique L'Autre Maison
54, avenue de la Motte-Picquet
75015 Paris, France
Phone 00 33 (0) 1 45 67 68 07
00 33 (0) 6 14 17 11 35

Page 142

Boutique Quattrocento
57, rue Georges Clémenceau
49150 Baugé, France
www.antiquitesquattrocento.com
antiquites.quattrocento@orange.fr

Page 156

Thierry Huau
Phone 00 33 (0) 6 07 59 78 10

Page 164

www.photosgourmandes.com
www.maboiteadiners.com

Page 172

Au Plaisir d'Antan
5, rue du Général Leclerc
95780 La Roche-Guyon, France
Phone 00 33 (0) 1 34 79 74 81
00 33 (0) 6 18 35 18 01

Page 182

Mathieu Leclercq
www.antiqleclercq.com
Phone 00 33 (0) 6 12 41 04 94

Espace Nord-Ouest
644, avenue du Général de Gaulle
59910 Bondues, France
Phone 00 33 (0) 3 20 03 38 39
www.nordouestantiquites.com

Page 202

Maison Caumont
23, rue Godefroy
93400 Saint-Ouen, France
Phone 00 33 (0) 1 75 34 60 02
00 33 (0) 6 03 48 23 02
www.maisoncaumont.com
caumont.laure@gmail.com

Page 212

Boutique Antiquités
4, place de l'Église
78113 Condé-sur-Vesgre, France
Phone 00 33 (0) 1 34 87 04 64
colette.jacoillot@orange.fr

Page 234

Boutique Det franska testamentet
Le Testament français
Upplandsgatan 36
11328 Stockholm, Sweden
Phone 00 46 (0) 8 32 33 67
martine@martinecolliander.com

Page 246

sverilhac@noos.fr

Page 256

Boutique Au Temps des Cerises
Phone 00 33 (0) 1 39 73 41 92
www.deco-autempsdescerises.com
autempsdescerises@orange.fr

Acknowledgments

The authors warmly thank all those who opened the doors of their homes and those who helped them to make this book a reality. In particular, thanks to Sophie Prételat, Annie Kuentzmann, and Mathieu Leclercq for their valuable support.

They would also like to express their gratitude to the Éditions de La Martinière team who helped produce this book: Isabelle Jendron, Laurence Basset, and Nathalie Mayevski.

Conception and production by Corinne Pauvert Thiounn

ENGLISH-LANGUAGE EDITION

Translated from the French by Amanda Katz

EDITOR: Laura Dozier
DESIGNER: Shawn Dahl, dahlimama inc
PRODUCTION MANAGER: Jules Thomson

Cataloging-in-Publication Data has been applied for and is available
from the Library of Congress.

ISBN: 978-0-8109-9867-4

© 2010 Éditions de la Martinière, an imprint of La Martinière Groupe, Paris
English translation © 2011 Abrams, New York

Originally published in French under the title *L'esprit XVIIIe aujourd'hui* by
Éditions de la Martinière, an imprint of La Martinière Groupe, Paris

Printed and bound in China
10 9 8 7 6 5 4 3 2 1

Abrams books are available at special discounts when purchased in quantity for
premiums and promotions as well as fundraising or educational use.
Special editions can also be created to specification. For details, contact
specialmarkets@abramsbooks.com or the address below.

THE ART OF BOOKS SINCE 1949

115 West 18th Street
New York, NY 10011
www.abramsbooks.com